We the Forest

ISBN 978-1-7393301-3-2

Published by Cultureshock
27B Tradescant Road
London SW8 1XD
cultureshock.com

Printed by Swallowtail Print

We the Forest

Written by
Sai Pathmanathan

Illustrated by
Sofia Iva

Contents

FORESTRY ENGLAND

Forestry England cares for more land and trees than any other organisation in the country – from small woodlands on the fringes of towns and cities, to vast areas such as the ancient New Forest. For more than 100 years we've been growing, shaping and caring for the nation's forests.

As well as creating vital habitats for wildlife, tackling climate change, and supplying sustainable home-grown timber, we provide beautiful and awe-inspiring places for people to enjoy.

Our longstanding contemporary art programme weaves together art, science, design, wellbeing and biodiversity to create amazing sculptures, installations, performances and exhibitions in magical forest settings, which rewild our imagination and build our connection with nature.

Forestry England: we are growing the future.

ABOUT THE AUTHOR

Sai Pathmanathan used to be a neuroscientist but moved into science communication and education because she loved creatively communicating science to all. She has worked in science education for more than 20 years, spanning nursery to postgraduate education. She now runs school workshops and afterschool science clubs, and writes books and resources to engage young people on the topics of food, health and the environment. Her book *Utterly Jarvellous* (Faber) won the 2021 Teach Primary Book Award for STEM.

ABOUT THE ILLUSTRATOR

Sofia Iva used watercolour as her main medium before working in digital art. Since completing a Bachelor of Arts degree in illustration, she has been creating digital artworks and developing illustrations for products, publishing, editorial, and advertising campaigns. She is currently based in Cyprus and finds her inspiration travelling to exotic parts of the world. Her delicate and refined handcrafted pieces are often inspired by nature and evoke a sense of curiosity and imagination.

Introduction

Forests need us and we need them. This book shows you the natural magic of forests and invites you to see the trees through new eyes – with the help of some artists. Artists and scientists have more in common than you would think. Before people could take photos, scientists had to be artists. They would look very closely at a leaf or a flower, then draw or paint it in beautiful detail. The next time you are in a forest, pay close attention and see if you can capture the wonder of trees in your own work of art.

Chapter 1

What makes a forest?

Magical forests

Forests are places of magic in fairy tales. They are also magical in very real ways. Forests are where trees send secret messages to each other, where sunlight turns into food, and where rare animals hide. Forests are home to 80% of the world's plants and animals (humans included). Growing in a community, trees protect each other, and together can even make their own weather. Beneath their protecting branches we can find food and water, and take shelter from extreme heat and cold.

Under cover

Some forests have thick canopies, which means their upper branches and leaves overlap, making a perfect home for owls and other wildlife by day or night.

More than three billion people around the world live within 1km of a forest

In this image from a film by Barbadian artist **Versia Harris**, *They Say You Can Dream A Thing More Than Once*, Swan Girl travels through the forest in her quest to transform into a princess, finding wonderful things along the way. Many works of art, stories and songs are set in the woods. Forests can be anything to us – a place where we, and our imaginations, can run free.

Create an artwork of what a forest would look like in your dreams.

How do forests form?

Bare rock can be turned into a forest, but this magic trick takes hundreds of years. Lichens, mosses and what we call pioneer plants – such as the ones you see trying to grow between paving stones – are the first to arrive. They break down rock, opening the way for grasses, ferns and herbs. Taller, woody shrubs can start to grow next, shading the ground and protecting other plants and animals. As plants die and rot into the ground, the soil deepens and becomes richer. Later, small trees with shorter lives form a young forest. After more time passes, these trees are replaced by long-living trees that age into an old forest. The forest never stops changing.

First to last

Pioneer species are followed by grasses. Then shrubs and hardy trees, like pines, can grow. Lastly, long-living trees, such as oak, arrive. These different stages are called a succession, and a single forest can be a patchwork of different stages at once.

Rock on

Lichens grow very slowly – only about the length of a pencil point in a year – but they can turn rock into soil. They release acid that makes tiny cracks in the rocks, which the lichen then grows into.

Forests everywhere

Forests grow all around. There are three main types: tropical, temperate and boreal. Tropical forests, such as the Amazon rainforest, are found on the equator, where it is always warm and rainy. Temperate forests grow where the temperature changes with the seasons and winters are not very harsh. These forests have deciduous trees – trees that lose their leaves in autumn. Some temperate forests have evergreen trees, which keep their leaves all year round. Boreal forests are found only in areas with high snowfall and short summers, surviving freezing winters. These forests have mostly evergreen trees. On mountains, the 'tree line' is the point above which trees will not grow because it is too high and cold.

Adapting well

Mangrove trees can survive in seawater by filtering out the salt. Pine trees in the icy north have needles for leaves with waxy coats to protect them from frost.

Forests once covered about half of the land on Earth – they now cover about a third

Derek Tumala's artwork *Kayamanan ng Pilipinas (Treasures of the Philippines)* is displayed on a TV screen and shows a tropical forest scene that changes with the real weather outside. On a wet day, the plants are showered with rain. When the sun

comes out, the vegetation shines gloriously too. This work celebrates natural resources – our true treasures – and makes us think about how changing weather affects them.

Draw a forest that gets too much sunshine and no water.

Hollow centre

Sometimes when a tree's bark is damaged, the dead heartwood inside can rot away, leaving a woody cave where animals can make their homes.

Inside a tree

If we slice through a tree trunk, we can see five different layers. Outer bark protects the tree on the outside, like the way our skin protects us. Inner bark is made of tubes (called phloem), which take sugary sap from the leaves to the rest of the tree. The next layer is the growing part of the tree (cambium) and if it is damaged the tree will slowly die. The middle of the trunk is made of tubes that take water and minerals up the tree from the roots like drinking straws. These living tubes, called xylem or sapwood, surround older, dead sapwood. This sapwood no longer carries water. Instead it forms a solid core in the heart of the tree, which makes it stand tall and strong.

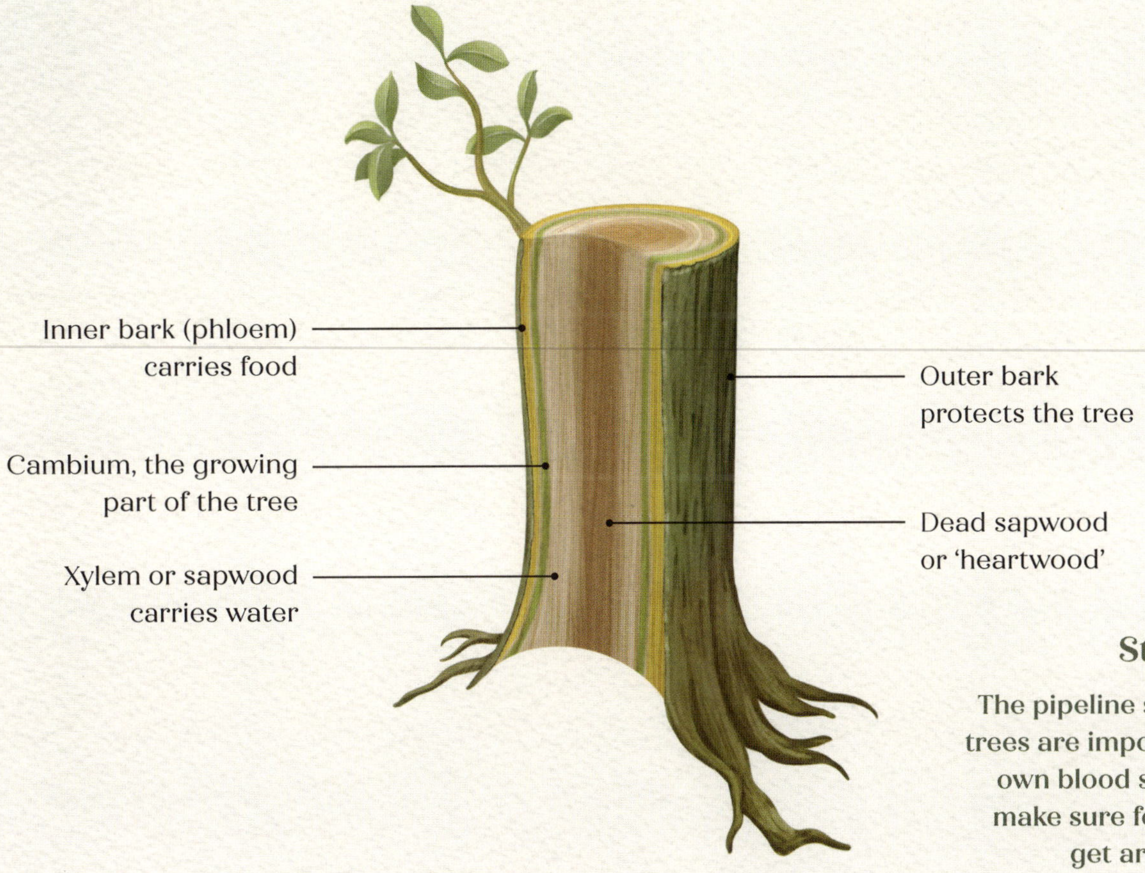

Staying alive

The pipeline systems inside trees are important, like our own blood systems – they make sure food and water get around the tree.

Photosynthesis: a light snack

Trees and plants do not exactly eat sunlight, but they do need it to make their food. Trees take in water through their roots, and carbon dioxide gas from the air through their leaves. They then use the energy from sunlight to break up the water and carbon dioxide in a chemical reaction to form glucose. This is a kind of sugar that plants use as food to help them grow. Oxygen is left over after they do this and plants release it from their leaves into the air. This is perfect for us, as we and other animals need oxygen to breathe.

The roots of life

The special ability of plants to make their own food using sunlight's energy is what makes them the first step in any food chain – and essential to life on Earth.

Good to be green

As sunlight hits the leaf's surface, the energy is captured by chlorophyll, a substance in plants that gives leaves their green colour.

All the oxygen on Earth has been made by photosynthesis, which began around 3.5 billion years ago

All shapes and sizes

There are more than 73,000 species of tree in the world. So how do we tell them apart? With a bit of detective work. Once we get to know trees, we can recognise them from their outlines. We can also examine the bark of trees. One of the best clues, though, is to look at the leaves of a tree. Leaves come in a huge variety of shapes – such as needles, fans, ovals and hearts – as well as textures, including furry, rough or waxy. These are often clever adaptations. Broad leaves, with their wavy edges, can curl up to avoid tearing in the wind or overheating in the sun. Hairs on leaves can reflect sunlight or stop ice from forming directly on the leaves. The pointy drip tips on fleshy tropical leaves allow the rainwater to run off them, so that they do not rot.

The fan shape of ginkgo leaves remains almost unchanged after 200 million years

Leaf line-up

Identify your leaf! The blades of simple leaves, such as those of the elm, are in one piece. Compound leaves are divided into leaflets, like those of the rowan tree.

Apple
Beech
Cedar
Dogwood
Elm
Fir
Ginkgo
Horse chestnut
Ilex
Juniper
Kentucky coffeetree
Linden
Mulberry
Nannyberry
Oak
Pine
Quaking aspen
Redwood
Sycamore
Tree of heaven
Umbrella tree
Viburnum
Weeping willow
Xanthoxylum
Yellowwood
Zelkova

Irish artist **Katie Holten** is famous for her *Tree Alphabets* – secret languages that use the silhouettes of different species of trees instead of letters. Here, we have A for apple tree, B for beech tree, and so on. Below is a poem, translated from a Japanese haiku by Matsuo Bashō, written in tree. Can you translate it using the alphabet on the left? (Answer on page 119)

More tree letters are hidden on pages within this book for you to find. Put them together to spell out the mystery word. (Answer on page 119)

Write a secret message in tree and ask friends to work it out.

Trees on the move

Trees cannot walk to new places, but as the climate changes, trees might slowly adapt where they live, such as shifting further north or higher up a mountain. We can help by planting trees suited to new conditions.

Tree travellers

Native trees are trees that have always grown in a place. In the UK, we think of native trees as those that have grown here since the last Ice Age, about 11,000 years ago. Some common trees seen in the UK today are not native, such as the horse chestnut. Although trees can spread to other areas by sending out their seeds, it is usually humans who bring plants from faraway places. Should we plant more non-native trees, if they can now survive in new areas in a changing climate? Maybe, but we have to be careful. Some are good for local wildlife, but others can cause problems, bringing pests or spreading quickly because no animals eat them. That can stop native trees from growing.

Cottonwood poplar seeds, shaped like tiny parachutes, can travel around 160km on the wind

Chapter 2

The forest as community

Can trees talk?

On a windy day we can hear trees make noises: the rustling of leaves or the creaking of branches. But have you ever wondered if trees talk to each other? Well they do, in a way. Scientific equipment has recorded trees making popping, clicking and crackling sounds when they need water or are damaged. Trees also use smells, which waft through the air to warn other trees of dangers – an animal munching on their leaves, for example. Tree communication can also happen below ground, between the roots of trees.

Trees are not loners but form friendly communities with their own species, as well as others

Scent by air

As a giraffe chews on an umbrella thorn acacia, the tree starts producing toxins in its leaves, which make animals sick. It also releases a warning gas so that nearby acacia trees make these poisons too, forcing the giraffe to feed on trees further away or on a different species.

Can a forest have a mind or its own intelligence? These are questions that **Ursula Biemann** asks in her video artwork *Forest Mind*, set in the Amazon forests of Colombia in South America. The artist looks at how the people who live there

communicate with the forest and the creatures in it. She also imagines seeing things from the forest's point of view.

Make a short video describing something clever in nature.

Fun guys

Fungi are not plants or animals. They grow but cannot make their own food like plants, and they contain chitin, which is also found in the bodies of insects.

Friendly fungi

Most of us think of the mushrooms we eat when we hear the word 'fungi'. But the parts we see above ground are just the fruit of fungi. Most of the fungi is underground. Some species of fungi are special and live closely together with trees. They have very fine threads that grow around or directly into a tree's root hairs. Trees share their sugars, made by photosynthesis, with their fungal friends. In exchange, the fungi help trees to take up water and minerals. They also protect them against toxins, disease and harmful fungi.

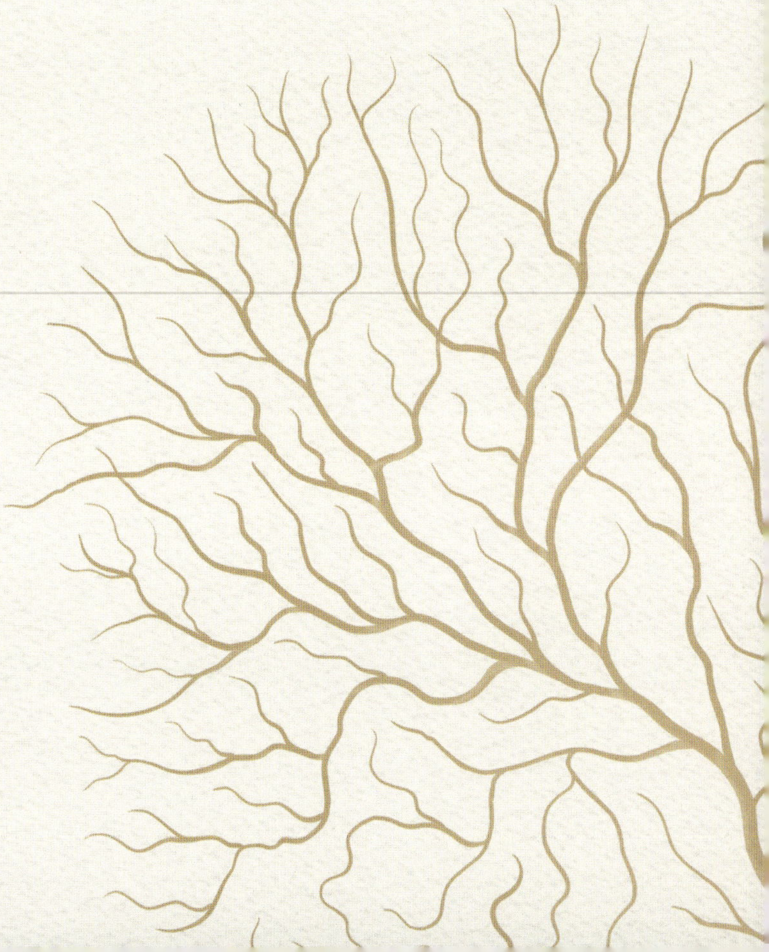

You can fit kilometres of fungal threads into one teaspoon of soil!

Underground network

Helpful fungi can link to more than one tree at the same time. They form a fungal network that connects trees up to one another. This network can cover huge distances underground. Through the fungal threads that connect their roots, trees of the same species can help each other by sharing sugars and water. They can also warn other trees about dangers, such as drought, disease or attacking insects.

Well connected

Tree stumps linked to other trees can be kept alive by these connections even when the stumps no longer have leaves to make their own food.

Barry Webb photographs fungi and slime moulds. Slime moulds are another tiny wonder of the forest community. They are not fungi or plants. Slime moulds also form networks, but they forage for food on trees and do not give back. Here you can see the slime mould *Arcyria denudata*, which grows no higher than 4mm – the thickness of two two-pence coins. One of its common names is Pink Carnival Candy Slime!

Fighting for light

Trees enjoy the perks of being cosy together in a forest. They shelter each other from storm winds, shade each other from the sun and help keep their surroundings at an even temperature. But they also have to fight for light, space and food. The birch tree, for example, has whip-like branches that stop others from growing into its space. Underground, trees can send out roots to steal water from their neighbours. Oak trees are often shadowed by beech trees. However, the mighty oak can survive out in the open alone, which not all trees can do.

A fatal hug

Strangler figs can grow from seeds left in bird droppings on other trees. They send out their roots and branches, wrapping around the host tree and eventually killing it.

Chapter 3

Life in the forest

Tree house

This fantasy tree shows a variety of animals from around the world. A tree can offer food for a sloth, a roost for a bat, a hiding place for a beetle and shelter for a fish, as well as a post for a bear to scratch messages on.

Home sweet home

Trees provide food and shelter for many creatures. By slowing down wind, and with their canopies acting like umbrellas, trees trap warm air. This keeps animals and birds cosy and dry in harsh weather. When it is scorchingly hot in the open, trees offer much-needed shade. For everything from the tiniest organisms, such as microbes and mites in the soil, to spiders, insects, reptiles and birds, trees are a life-giving source of food and the perfect habitat.

Oak trees, particularly ancient ones, can support more than 2,300 wildlife species

Mogajeguihu
Abel Rodriguez M

Abel Rodríguez is an artist and an elder of the Nonuya people from Colombia in South America. He knows all about the medicinal plants and wildlife of the Amazon and is called 'a namer of plants' by his community. Because of a war, the artist and his family had to leave their home. To keep his knowledge about the nature in his land alive, he paints images of the animals and trees, such as *Canangucha*l here, from his memory.

Draw a special tree from memory, showing all the details you can remember.

Tree defence

Have you ever noticed a tree with tough bark, branches lined with spiky thorns or leaves that are thick and waxy? These are all ways for trees to protect themselves from pest attacks or being grazed on. We have already seen how trees can warn each other through scent. But trees have yet another amazing talent. They can tell what is eating them and then use their scents to signal for help. Wasps and birds use their sense of smell to pick up on these adverts for a selection of juicy caterpillars!

Plants can change their chemical make-up, their taste and their smell in response to threats

Eating machines

Caterpillars, the larvae of butterflies and moths, can eat 100 times their own body mass in a day.

Forest friends

Many creatures are trees' little helpers without knowing it. Birds eat berries and other fruits and release the seeds in their poo – a ready-made compost – far away from the parent tree. This means that both the parent tree and young seedling can grow without competing with one another. Squirrels bury seeds, such as acorns, to eat later and sometimes forget about them, allowing new oaks to grow.

The African elephant transports seeds the furthest distance from the parent fruit tree... a whopping 65km away

Yew are amazing

Although the seeds are poisonous, badgers can swallow yew berries whole and poo them out. The seeds sprout and grow into new yew trees.

British artist **Levon Biss** makes amazingly detailed portraits of insects by taking thousands of close-up photographs and then stitching them all together. The finished pictures open our eyes to tiny things, such as the hairs on the legs of this *Tricoloured Jewel Beetle*. This wood-boring insect from Indonesia is an important food source for birds, and its larvae create tunnels that other insects and fungi use to live in.

Take a zoomed-in picture of an insect to see it in detail.

Tree shepherds

Although trees provide food for animals, they can also play a role in limiting their numbers, which helps to keep the forest in balance. For instance, during some years oak trees grow very few acorns. Although this might mean there are fewer oak seedlings, it also means fewer acorns for wild pigs (boars) to eat and so their numbers are kept low. Then, in years when oaks grow lots of acorns there are fewer boars to eat them, giving those seedlings a chance to grow. By having a supply of food that is different from year to year, the boars' population is kept in check and the forest stays healthy.

In some forests, acorns make up nearly three-quarters of a wild boar's diet

Nuts for acorns

Acorns are a highly nutritious food, which is why magpies, squirrels and boars love them.

Chapter 4

Change and survival

Thin, dark rings show the slower growth during late summer and autumn
Wood-boring larvae tunnel into the trunk
Wide, pale rings show spring and early summer growth
A lightning strike scorches the wood
The trunk shows wider rings where the tree has grown more on one side to keep itself upright on uneven ground
A forest fire damages the tree
The tree starts life as a seedling

Circle of life

The life story of a tree can be told through its rings. We can find clues to the times when the tree underwent hardship or damage, or had growth spurts during good times. A tree trunk's cross section tells us about how the tree has changed over time. Older trees keep growing, unlike humans who stop growing when still young. Ancient woodland trees also provide special habitats and a wondrous ecosystem for rare species of fungi and many creatures who call these trees home. So cutting down these older trees and replacing them with younger ones is not an equal trade.

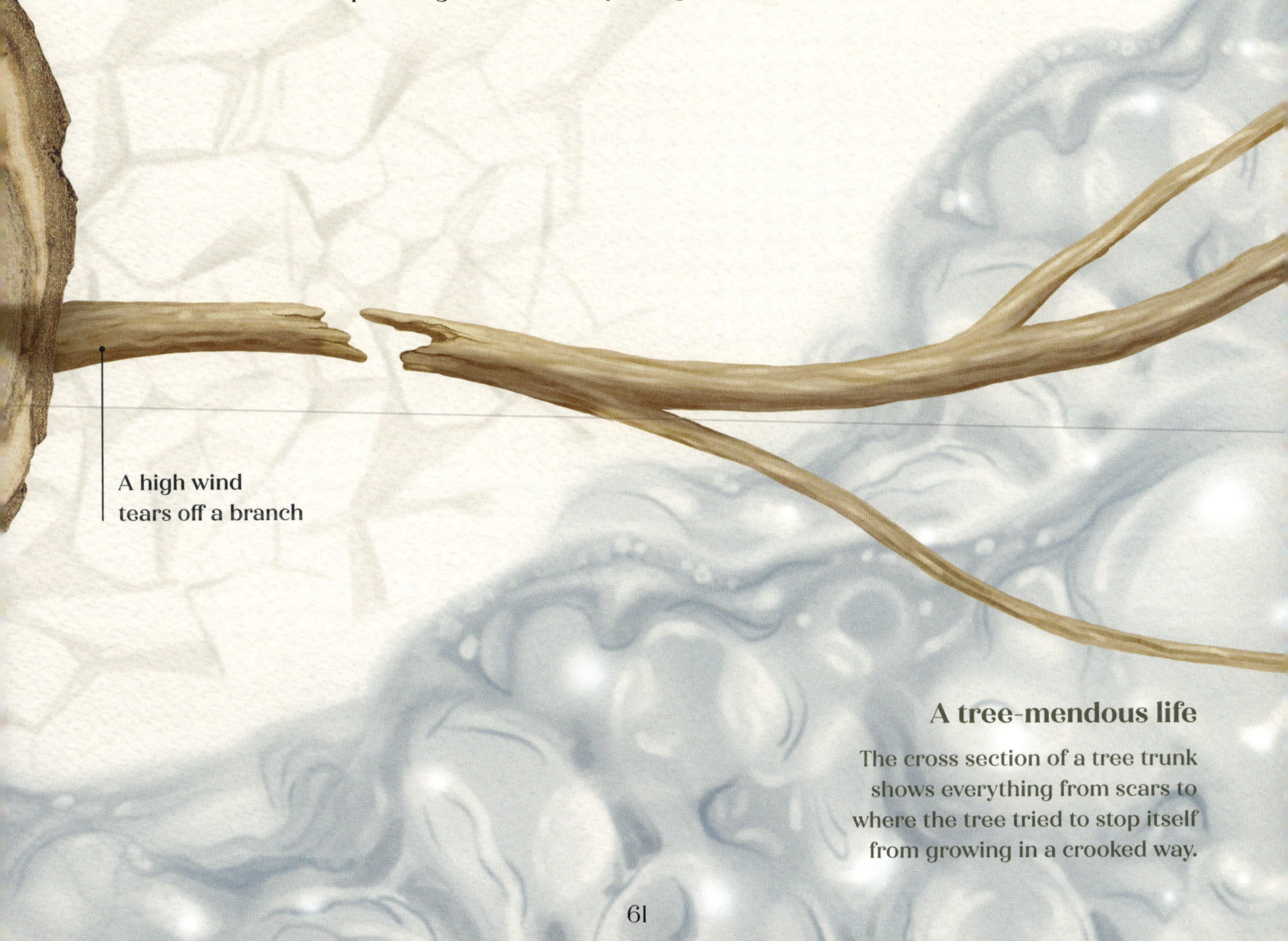

A tree-mendous life

The cross section of a tree trunk shows everything from scars to where the tree tried to stop itself from growing in a crooked way.

Losing leaves

It is autumn! Brightly coloured leaves adorn deciduous trees, ready to drop. During these cooler, darker days there is less sunlight for leaves. The pigment chlorophyll, which makes leaves green, breaks down and the tree absorbs the useful nutrients. Other colours are now revealed – reds, oranges or yellows. At the base of each leaf, a special layer of cells grows to cut the leaf off from its twig without leaving an open wound. Deciduous trees drop their leaves because these freeze in winter and cannot make food. A leafless tree also catches less wind, so it is less likely to blow over in a storm.

Be-leaf it

All the chlorophyll in a plant cell is found in the chloroplasts, which are tiny parts within the plant cells.

Too soon

This muddled tree shows four seasons in one day. A cherry blossom flowers while the snow has not yet melted, but this provides much-needed nectar for insects.

Tree o'clock

As the planet warms, all plants, including trees, can become a little confused. Milder winters, hotter summers, and too much or not enough rain means that trees have to try to adapt. Chemicals in the tree are released at different times, based on the tree's environment. These determine when a tree loses its leaves, starts to bud or continues fruiting. If it is time for a tree to get ready for winter but the days are still warm, the tree could bud again. Creatures that depend on trees then start to match their behaviours, such as building nests, to what the trees are providing.

In winter, many trees go dormant – they are still alive but are not growing

Create a mesmerising outdoor artwork using only natural materials.

One Tree Four Seasons is an art project between architect/artist **Ulf Mejergren** and artist **Antti Laitinen** in Sweden. They collected fallen branches and leaves to create a woven nest around an old alder tree growing just outside Stockholm. Four variations of the work tell us about each season. In *Season III*, the third image, collected leaves were blown into the structure artificially, but the wind blew them out again – showing the beauty of the human-made meeting the natural.

Growing back

Just as we grow new skin cells for our protection, tree bark continues to grow. If the bark gets damaged, the tree can become infected, which affects its ability to take in food and water. Trees cannot stick a plaster on the hurt area to heal themselves, but they can seal off the wound and grow around it to stay healthy. Trees can regrow bark so well that it is often impossible to tell where a branch was once shed. Some trees are also able to grow a new tree from a cut branch or 'cutting'.

Healing tears

Some trees, such as eucalyptus, weep sap when injured or attacked by insects in order to defend themselves and prevent infection.

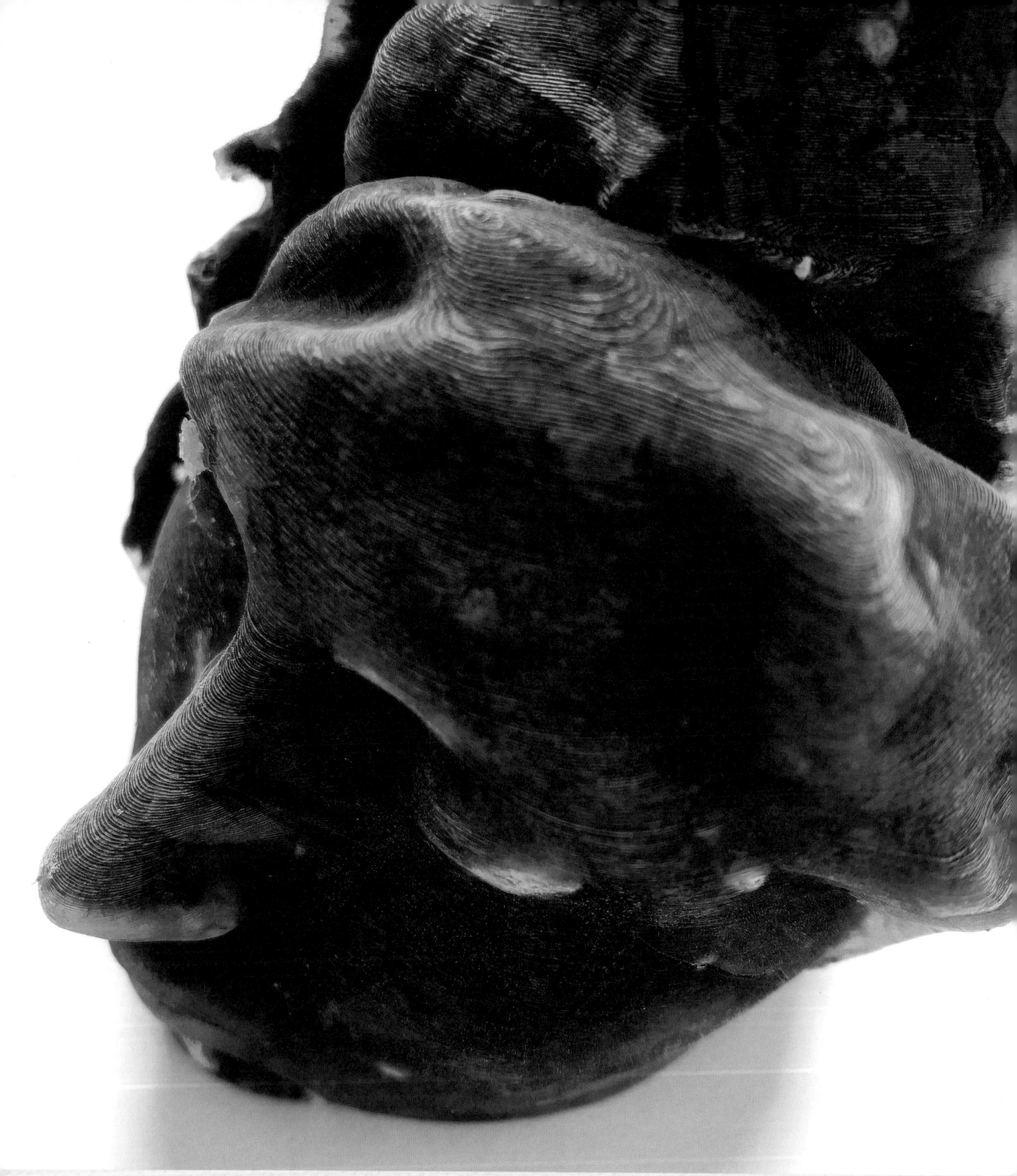

Becky Lyon's eerie artwork *Compost Crystals* explores the question of whether dead logs are really dead. As log piles rot down, insects, fungi, mosses and lichens move in, leading Lyon to ask: 'Who's who in the rot?' She freezes compost and water,

then sculpts it into shapes based on logs, forest floor debris and parts of herself. When her icy work melts, she remakes it.

Make your own log pile with pieces of tree trunk, branches and twigs to create a natural habitat for insects and fungi.

Life after death

A new beginning

A sapling grows in the centre of a lake on a nurse log, which gives it nutrients and a place to root.

There is no life without death. Without dead wood in forests, the ecosystem would fall apart. The vital nutrients within decaying wood can feed fungi and insects, as well as help new trees to grow strong. This is why keeping a tidy natural environment will not encourage more wildlife. Leaving trees where they fall, or allowing dead ones to stand where they are, provides perfect homes for birds, beetles and much more wildlife. This way food chains remain intact. For example, woodpeckers can eat insects that feed on dead wood.

New tree saplings can sprout on 'nurse logs', which are fallen or dying trees

Forests in danger

Forests face many distressing issues right now. As the human population grows, farming and the need for timber grows too. Storms and floods in some areas, and huge wildfires in others, are causing the loss of trees. This, in turn, causes ecosystems to crumble and many species of wildlife to disappear. Replacing forests with fields or buildings, burning fossil fuels (such as coal or gas), and making cement cause much of the rise in carbon dioxide in the air. This traps heat in Earth's atmosphere, warming the planet at an alarming rate.

About a third of the world's conifer species are at risk of extinction

High and dry

Losing forests can lead to drought. Without trees to trap moisture and hold the soil together with their roots, the land gets drier.

Rising from the ashes

When wildfires burn out of control, it is terrifying for those with homes in the area, whether humans or animals. But some trees, such as the conifer species lodgepole pine, have 'sleeping seeds' that need extreme heat to trigger growth. And the ashes that result from a fire are a perfect fertiliser. Other trees, such as giant sequoias, have adapted to seasonal fires by developing thick, fire-resistant bark. However, there is now a huge increase in extreme wildfires, driven by the climate crisis. If this carries on we may lose more forest than can regenerate.

After the fire

Some burnt and seemingly dead trees can spring back to life once a wildfire is over.

Here we see a photograph from American artist **Jeff Frost**'s time-lapse film *California on Fire*. Frost trained as a firefighter so he could experience first-hand what it was like to be at the heart of the devastating wildfires that swept across the American West in 2019. He filmed the flames spreading over the beautiful forested landscape, creating a moving reminder that we need to protect our precious planet from the effects of climate change. One way of doing this is to look after these forests better by copying methods used by the Indigenous peoples who have lived on the land for thousands of years.

Chapter 5

Why are forests precious?

Pipe up!

This huge sculpture by Russian artist Nikolay Polissky is as high as two houses and made from woven birch twigs.

Wood from the trees

Trees inspire us to be creative, and they also give us wood for furniture, timber for buildings, and paper for art and learning. Where would we be without books? Building with wood is good for the planet if it is taken from forests that are managed well. It is much less harmful for the environment than building with concrete or steel, which release lots of carbon dioxide when they are made. Building with wood does not result in these high levels of harmful gases. Trees also capture carbon from the air while they grow, and wooden buildings keep that carbon stored inside them.

Wooden buildings can be as strong as ones made of concrete or steel

Helen Sear's *Becoming Forest* is a series of pictures that captures the experience of being inside a forest. *Becoming Forest 4* (above) and *5* (above right) show the neon 'graffiti tags' left by foresters to mark which trees to cut or leave standing. The artist later added her own colourful tracings to the photographs, highlighting

details of trees down to the tiniest twigs. Sear observes how everything in the forest ecosystem interweaves as she forms rich, tapestry-like artworks.

Some cities, such as London, have enough trees to be called a forest

Forests can fight pollution

Trees make the oxygen we need to breathe and can also filter harmful pollutants from the air in cities. Air pollution can cause health problems, but trees and plants can trap polluting particles on their leaves. Hairy, rough and waxy leaves are particularly good at this. Trees can also clean water through their roots. City environments can be tough for trees though. They are often planted surrounded by tarmac and where they are unable to connect to other trees. We should fill our cities with trees and care for them well – they take care of us too.

City forest

In many cities, trees are planted along roads, as well as in parks and elsewhere, to help keep air clean and provide vital shade. The more trees the better!

How trees cool the planet

Trees really are cool! Sitting in the shade of a tree is the perfect way to hide from the scorching sun. Tree canopies trap 90% of the heat from the sun and can chill the ground below them by about 12°C. In cities, dark tarmac roads and buildings soak up heat during the day and release it at night. This is called the 'urban heat island effect', and cities can be 3-4°C hotter than the greener places around them. Planting trees in cities can make them much cooler.

Transpiration is a tree's way of sweating, which can cool them, and us, down

Making rain

Water vapour rises from forests and joins clouds, which causes more rain to fall in the area.

Slowing down floods

All plants need water. When there is too much rain, trees and plants can directly soak it up with their roots and store it. They also help in other ways. Leafy tree crowns and rough trunks can trap water and slow rainfall down. Some rainwater can also evaporate from plants back into the air, without ever hitting the ground. Tree roots hold the soil together, while also creating air channels where water can travel downwards. Water is sponged up by the soil and stored as groundwater, making it less likely to cause floods or landslides.

Drip drip

Broad leaves can trap rainwater, slowing its journey to the ground, and giving groundwater time to drain away.

Gather your friends to celebrate trees through a dance performance.

Here we see a banyan tree dancer, Nur Roqim, in a performance called *Rippling Water, Spreading Roots* by British artist **Ella Chedburn**, working with several Indonesian artists, including the arts collective **Gulung Tukar**. The dance was inspired by the ritual of Ringin Kurung, held centuries ago when seven banyan trees were planted to soak up floodwater in the Indonesian city of Tulungagung. Other people joined Roqim as mystical creatures in the ritual, working together to make the water retreat and celebrating the delicate balance between water and earth.

Soothing green

Being in a green environment, such as a forest, makes us slow down, reducing our heart rate so that we feel less stressed and more peaceful.

Calming trees

We know that being outdoors is good for our mental health and wellbeing, but why? 'Phyto' means 'plant' in Greek, and phytochemicals are chemicals that plants make to kill off bad fungi, bacteria and viruses – anything that can cause disease. These plant-made chemicals happen to be good for us too. Terpenes are a phytochemical made by plants, and conifers in particular. They can calm our anxious minds and even cure illness. This is why walking in a pine forest, breathing in these natural smells, can help us stay healthy.

This photo – *Beatriz* by artist **Liv Milani** – is of Beatriz Cauper Garcia. A grandmother of 12, she is a *vegetalista*, a traditional healer of the Shipibo-Conibo people of the Peruvian Amazon rainforest. Her father taught her ancestral healing practices, and the Amazon jungle is her pharmacy. The majestic fig tree she leans against here (*Ficus insipida*) has a milky sap with many medicinal uses. When we look after the rights of the women of the Amazon rainforest, we also protect the forest.

Find a tree and take a self-portrait with it.

Give it a whorl

The spirals or whorls in ferns repeat and get smaller and smaller. These repeating patterns are known as fractals and are extremely calming to look at.

Fascinating forests

Some of our happiest moments are spent outdoors, relaxing in wild settings or walking through a leafy forest. The repeated patterns we see in nature, such as symmetries, catch our attention in a gentle way. We notice large tree branches dividing into smaller branches, and the spirals of snail shells, ferns or sunflowers. These awe-inspiring patterns fascinate us and relax our minds. This is why after a short break in nature our minds feel refreshed and ready to focus on our tasks again. Looking at screens cannot restore our minds in this way.

Happiness Beyond Paradise is a work by Brazilian artist **Luiz Zerbini**. He is inspired by the enchanting landscapes and lush vegetation of his country, and also by the mathematical order of geometry. His grid looks a little like a mosaic, or the front of a tower block. This work is three metres high and six metres wide, and the artist

wants people who look at it to feel that they might be standing in a real forest. His swirls and patterns also provide a feeling of movement, like trees in the wind.

Use natural materials from outdoors to create a mosaic that represents 'happiness'.

The forest inside of us

Just as forests are an ecosystem – one where trees create a habitat for many creatures – we too have an ecosystem inside us. We contain a multitude of tiny creatures called microbes, too small to be seen with the naked eye. In fact, our bodies are made up of slightly more microbes than human cells! The bacteria, viruses and fungi that live in and on our bodies are together called a 'microbiome' – a tiny world. As they do in the forest, microbes can harm or help us. Good gut bacteria, for instance, help us to digest our food. Microbes are so tiny they can enter and leave our skin when we touch things, so we are more a part of the world than we realise.

We are one

The forest outside is a joined-up ecosystem of beings: plants, animals, fungi and more. We too are part of this forest.

Double Plot is a huge tapestry by Nigerian/Belgian artist **Otobong Nkanga**. She makes art about how we damage Earth by cutting down trees and mining for precious metals. In this tapestry, silvery lines look like veins or a map, and behind them is a view of the galaxy. A figure on the left pulls strings, just like we control the fate of our planet. On the right, six arms attempt to move things, perhaps

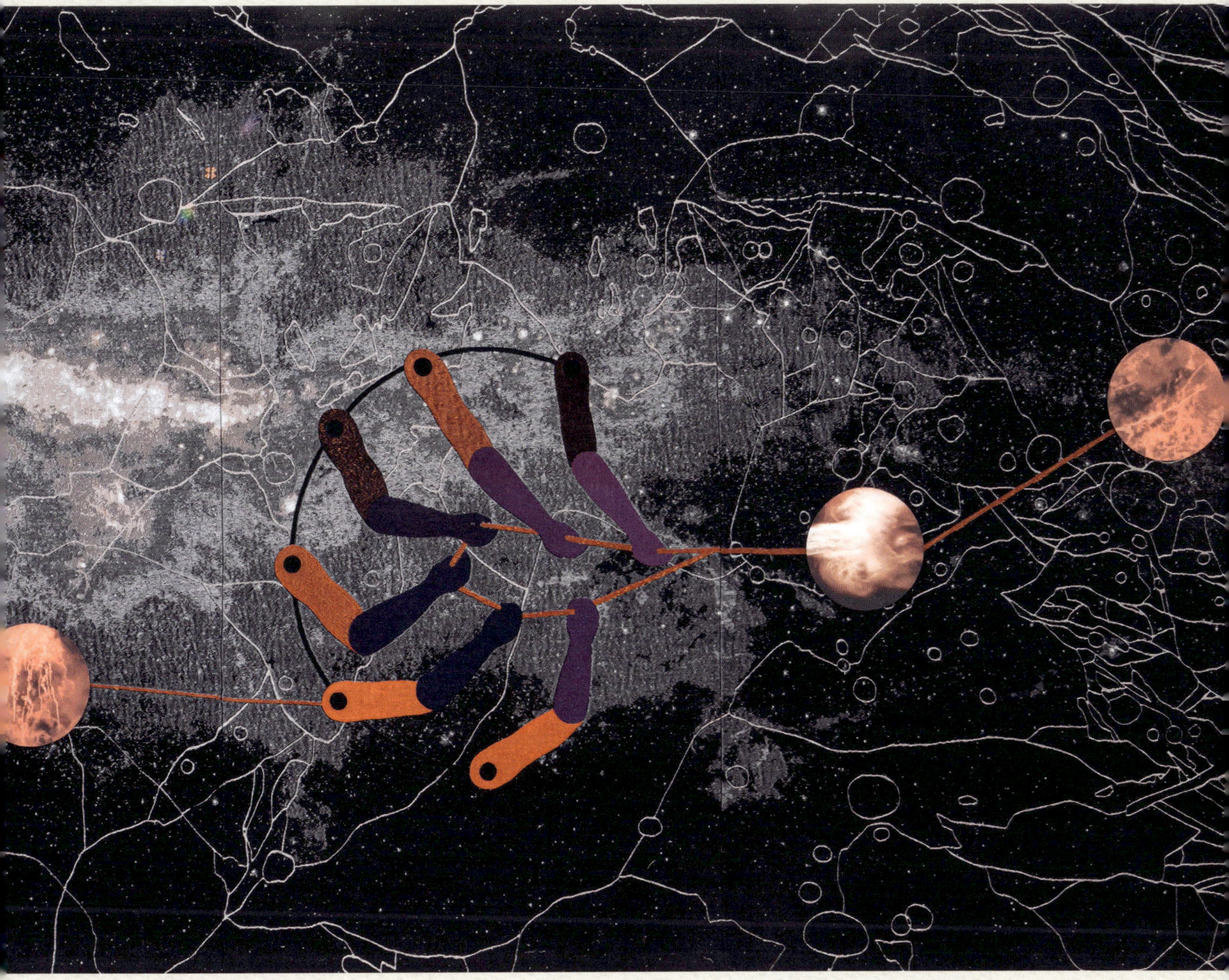

Write your own inspirational quote about how connected you feel to nature.

in a different direction. Our actions have an effect, and everything is connected. Otobong says: 'Food systems, water bodies and trees, all the things that are around us, they should be things we care for, because without them we cannot even exist.'

Chapter 6

Forests of the future

Protecting the forest

Trees are under threat from a changing climate, drought, floods, and new pests and diseases. In some places, they are cut down to make way for farmland and not regrown. Where we manage forests properly we can protect them, and plan which trees to grow and which to remove. Animals such as elephants and beavers also fell trees, and these natural processes are important as they open up the woodland, letting light through so flowers can grow. It is important to choose the right trees when planting them in their new homes – different trees in the mountains, by the wet banks of rivers or in dry savannas. You can talk to others about forests and support nature reserves, treating trees with care when you visit them. You can even plant a tree in your local community.

Safe from harm

Our beautiful forests are too vast to cover with a glass dome, but we can protect them in other ways.

Bring it back

Native animals, such as wild ponies, can be put back into the environment to graze, forage and trample. This creates habitats for other wildlife.

How to grow more forests

'Reforesting' is about planting more trees where they have been lost. But we need to plant a mix of the right species if we want strong forests for today and the future. While we can turn farmland back into woodland, we should not add trees just anywhere – for example, on rare grasslands or in deep peat bogs. Helping to return land to its natural state, along with the animals that used to live there, is called 'rewilding'. Beavers, which make natural dams, and European bison, which change the landscape with their grazing, are examples of animals that have a big effect on ecosystems. Bringing back nature in this way can transform our landscapes and help solve climate change.

Right tree, right place, right reason...

This sports stadium in Austria was temporarily transformed into a forest using 300 native trees by the Swiss artist **Klaus Littmann**. His work was called *FOR FOREST – The Unending Attraction of Nature*, and people who sat in the stadium could watch

the beautiful landscape changing with the weather, season and light. Where else might we grow forests in the future?

Close your eyes and imagine a forest around a famous landmark.

Fantasy forests

Imagine trees floating up in the sky, out of reach. In what amazing place could you picture growing a dream forest?

Forests of the imagination

Forests are mysterious places, full of leafy hiding places to explore. You can find sticks that could be wands or wizards' staffs, or part of a den. Spending time in the forest lets our minds wander in different ways. Can you imagine if there were forests all around? What if we could bring forests to our cities – on streets, up the sides of buildings and even on rooftops? At the moment, only one fifth of Earth's forests remain undisturbed. Imagine if they were all thriving.

This is an image from a video called *Sanctuary of the Unseen Forest*, which is shown on a huge screen. It was made by the art group **Marshmallow Laser Feast** with **Andres Roberts** and **James Bulley**. As we watch the video we seem to float around a majestic

kapok tree (*Ceiba pentandra*) from the Amazon, and see right inside it to the living roots. It makes us feel wonder at the deep link between trees and ourselves.

Draw a diagram of your place within nature.

Artist biographies

In order of appearance in the book

Versia Harris is an artist who lives and works in Barbados. Her art explores fantasy, dreams and wishes, examining ideas around our collective fantasies about ourselves, our nations and our world. She teaches at The Barbados Community College and her work is shown in international exhibitions.

Derek Tumala is a visual artist from the Philippines who works with new and emerging technologies, moving images, industrial materials and objects. His art involves science, nature and, in particular, the idea of interconnectedness.

Katie Holten is an Irish artist, activist and bestselling author. Her work investigates the entangled relationships between humans and the natural world. She has created *Tree Alphabets*, a *Stone Alphabet*, and a *Wildflower Alphabet* to share the joy she finds in her love of the more-than-human world.

Ursula Biemann is a Swiss video artist and author whose art involves fieldwork, often in Indigenous territories, and making connections between different kinds of knowledge. She is interested in the political ecologies of forests, oil and water, and looking at alternative environmentally friendly ways of relating to the natural world. Her book *Forest Mind* examines the interconnection of all life.

Barry Webb is an award-winning photographer and a fellow of the Royal Photographic Society. He specialises in ultra-macro photography, and has a particular interest in slime moulds and fungi. He contributes records for local and national databases. His images have been exhibited and published in many countries.

Abel Rodríguez was born in the Colombian Amazon jungle where his knowledge about plants led to him becoming known as a 'namer of plants'. After fleeing violence in the jungle to live in the Colombian city of Bogotá, he helped biologists studying Amazon plants with his expertise and drawings of plants, going on to create artworks that are shown worldwide.

Levon Biss is a British artist who is widely regarded as one of the leading macro photographers of his generation. He describes his artworks primarily as educational tools that encourage the appreciation of the natural world. His high-magnification photos are used in school curriculums around the globe and his exhibitions present microscopic worlds to audiences, enabling them to appreciate details normally invisible to the human eye.

Antti Laitinen works with photography, sculpture, video, performance, installation and conceptual objects. He is inspired by taking apart and then rethinking and rebuilding his everyday environment, to make us reflect on our relationship with our environment.

Ulf Mejergren is a Swedish artist and architect who creates temporary structures using natural materials. His work is a mixture of architecture, art and nature, bringing together the logic of architecture, the whimsical spirit of art and the freedom of nature.

Becky Lyon is an English/Jamaican artist based in London who uses art to connect with ecology. This inspires her installations, sculpture, sensory materials, moving images and photographic objects. She is the founder of Ground Provisions – an artist-led, schooled-by-the-forest for grown-ups – and is a volunteer London National Park City Ranger.

Jeff Frost is an artist in California working to reconnect humans to nature through time, sound, photography, painting, and film. His work has appeared in museums, exhibitions and film festivals worldwide, and he was a subject of *Fire Chasers* on Netflix.

Helen Sear is a British artist who specialises in photography and moving images. Her art is about how humans, animals and natural environments coexist. She was the first woman to represent Wales with a solo exhibition at the 56th Venice Biennale in 2015 with her works *...the rest is smoke*. Her works are in many public and private collections and she has exhibited her art internationally.

Ella Chedburn is a British artist who merges nature, technology and mysticism. Her work has ranged from mischievous plants wired to computers, to playful guides about herbal medicine for virtual reality. The forest is a recurring setting for her work as she navigates its ancient, mystical roots in relation to the radically technologised world surrounding it.

Gulung Tukar is an arts collective based in the city of Tulungagung in Indonesia. The group supports lots of different artworks created by all kinds of people working together. Gulung Tukar stands against inequality and aims to create more healthy and equal environments.

Liv Milani is an artist and award-winning photographer based in the UK. She is the founder of the art project *Women and Trees*, which aims to raise awareness about the environment and highlight the role of women in restoring our connection to nature. Milani believes that art is a powerful healing force, inspiring positive change and activating the imagination. Through visual storytelling, she invites us to remember ourselves as nature.

Luiz Zerbini is a Brazilian artist known for his vivid works on canvas, which range from abstract paintings to landscapes, cityscapes and domestic scenes. Using natural and geometric forms, his paintings explore the relationship between colour, light and movement. He tries to provide the impression of 'being in the painting as you could be in a forest'. His work has featured in major solo exhibitions in Brazil and is shown internationally.

Otobong Nkanga is an award-winning Belgian/Nigerian artist whose art examines the ways that bodies, territories, minerals and the earth relate to each other. Through drawing, installation, performance, photography, tapestry and sculpture, Nkanga makes connections between the natural world and themes such as memory, labour, home, care, ownership, emotion, touch and smell. Her work looks at how connection can move us towards a more liveable future. She exhibits her work in solo international exhibitions.

Klaus Littmann is an artist, curator and producer based in Basel, Switzerland. He is known for his solo and group art exhibitions in public spaces in cities, and is interested in the confrontation between contemporary art and urban spaces. He was awarded the Culture Prize of the City of Basel in 2002.

Marshmallow Laser Feast is a London-based collective of artists working where science, art and technology meet, inviting participants to use their senses to navigate beyond the everyday. The collective makes work with artists, scientists, poets, musicians, programmers and engineers to 'leave a slug trail of sensory experiences'.

Andres Roberts is a British guide, educator and leadership advisor, and founder of the Bio-Leadership Project.

James Bulley is a British artist and composer whose work explores sound, space and the more-than-human world.

Glossary

Ancient woodland – in the UK, woodland that has been in continuous existence since 1600 (1750 in Scotland).

Boreal – northern regions with long winters and short, cool summers, usually with mostly coniferous forests.

Broadleaf – trees that do not have needles or cones, such as oak, birch and beech.

Cambium – a thin layer of cells between the **xylem** and **phloem** layers in plants, from which new cells of wood and bark grow.

Carbon dioxide – a gas naturally found in air. Plants take it in during **photosynthesis**.

Carbon sequestration – long-term storage of carbon in trees and other organisms, soil and oceans. It can also be done artificially.

Conifers – trees with needles and cones, such as spruce, pine and larch.

Chlorophyll – a pigment in green plants that enables light to be absorbed to provide energy for **photosynthesis**.

Compound leaf – a leaf where the blade is divided, forming leaflets.

Deciduous – a tree or plant that sheds its leaves each year.

Ecosystem – an area where plants, animals and other organisms, as well as weather and landscapes, interact.

Evergreen – a tree or plant that keeps its leaves for more than one growing season.

Forester – a person who is in charge of taking care of a forest.

Fractals – a pattern that repeats forever, where every part of it looks very similar to the whole image.

Habitat – an area that provides an animal or plant with adequate food, water, shelter and living space in a suitable arrangement.

Hardwood – the wood of broadleaf trees, such as oak, birch and beech; or the broadleaf trees themselves.

Microbes – tiny living things that are too small to be seen without a microscope.

Mycorrhizal fungi – the name for the 'friendly' fungi that link to plants' roots and help them take up water and nutrients and, in turn, receive some of the sugars those plants make through **photosynthesis**.

Phloem – the cells in plants that carry the sugars made during **photosynthesis** from the leaves to storage areas – seeds and fruits. It also carries sugars to parts of the plants that are growing, such as the roots.

Photosynthesis – the chemical process carried out by green plants in the presence of light, which combines carbon dioxide from the atmosphere with hydrogen from water in the soil to form sugars as food for the growing plant. Oxygen is a by-product of the reaction.

Phytochemicals – natural chemicals that are found in plants.

Sapwood (also called **xylem**) – the young sap-containing and usually lighter-coloured wood found just beneath the bark of a tree.

Simple leaf – a leaf with a single blade.

Softwood – the wood of coniferous trees, such as spruce, pine and larch; a term sometimes used for the coniferous trees themselves.

Species – a set of animals or plants in which the members have similar characteristics to each other and can breed with each other.

Sustainable forest management – managing forests to meet the needs of the present without harming the ability of future generations to meet their needs.

Temperate – a region with mild temperatures and moderate rainfall.

Timber harvest – removing trees from a forest to restore its health or to create sustainable forest products such as timber for building or wood products.

Transpiration – the process by which water is pulled from the roots of the plant through the stems and leaves and then released through microscopic holes in the leaves called stomata.

Tropical – a region with warm temperatures through the year and lots of rain.

Woodland – land under stands of trees with a canopy cover of at least a fifth.

Xylem – see **sapwood**.

We hope you found the secret *Tree Alphabet* word in this book. The answer is:
ACORN

The poem on page 27 reads:
Old pond
Frog leaps in
Waters sound

Credits

With thanks to the following people at Forestry England
Nick Bryant, Stuart Burgess, Alice Cheyne, Tom Dearnley, Louise Fedotov-Clements, Jodie Green, Marie Howden, Dr Lucie Jerabkova, Josephine Lavelle, Kate Nixon, Mike Seddon, Hayley Skipper, Hazel Stone, Dr Andrew Stringer, Dr Eleanor Tew, Nicola Withers and Sarah Wood

With thanks also to
Alex Morrison, Mariam Zulfiqar, James Hogan, Ewan Atkinson, Borbála Soós, Marie Perennès, Instituto de Visión, Lisson Gallery and Folio Art

Author
Sai Pathmanathan
Illustrator
Sofia Iva
Editor
Alison Sturgeon

Cultureshock
Head of creative: Tess Savina
Production editor: Claire Sibbick
Designer: Ieva Misiukonytė
Chief executive: Phil Allison
Managing director: Patrick Kelly
Production manager: Nicola Vanstone
Copyeditor: Susie Wong
Proofreader: Debra Wolter

Photos

Cover	Westend61 GmbH/Alamy
8	Artem Evdokimov/Alamy
12	Versia Harris, still from *They Say You Can Dream A Thing More Than Once.* © Versia Harris
14	Grotmarsel/iStock
16	Yulia Kuznetsova/Alamy
18	Derek Tumala, still from *Kayamanan ng Pilipinas (Treasures of the Philippines).* © Derek Tumala
20	Roman Kýbus/Alamy
22	andDraw/iStock
24	Jose Hidalgo Richards/Alamy
26	Katie Holten, *Tree Alphabet*, 2015. © Katie Holten
28	Paula Dillinger/Alamy
30	Westend61 GmbH/Alamy
32	Sandra van der Steen/Alamy
34	Ursula Biemann, *Forest Mind*, 2021. © Ursula Biemann
36	Krailurk Warasup/Alamy
38	Mikel Martinez de Osaba/ Getty Images
40	© Barry Webb FRPS
44	Media Drum World/Alamy
46	yotrak/123RF
48	Image courtesy of Abel Rodríguez and Instituto de Visión. Photo: Maria Paula Bastidas
50	Shutterstock
52	Andrey Kuzmin/Alamy; Dreamstime
54	Levon Biss, *Tricoloured Jewel Beetle.* © Levon Biss
56	Mykola Davydenko/Alamy
58	Unsplash
60	Dreamstime
62	Robert Harding/Alamy
66	Ulf Mejergren and Antti Laitinen, stills from *One Tree Four Seasons*, 2022–23. © Ulf Mejergren and Antti Laitinen
68	Papilio/Alamy
70	Becky Lyon, *Compost Crystals*, 2021. © Becky Lyon
72	All Canada Photos/Alamy
74	Anna Kucherova/Alamy
76	Shutterstock
78	Jeff Frost, *California on Fire*, 2019. © Jeff Frost
80	Andrew Berezovsky/Alamy
82	Artwork by Nikolay Polissky; photo by Olga Simonova/Alamy
84	Helen Sear, *Becoming Forest 4* and *Becoming Forest 5*, 2017. © Helen Sear
86	Mockup Cloud
88	Allen Creative/Steve Allen/Alamy
90	Apisit Sriputtirut/Alamy
92	Ella Chedburn, *Rippling Water, Spreading Roots*, 2023. © Ella Chedburn
94	Shutterstock
96	Liv Milani, *Beatriz*, 2023. © Liv Milani
98	Dreamstime
100	Luiz Zerbini, *Happiness Beyond Paradise*, 2020. © Luiz Zerbini. Courtesy of the artist; Stephen Friedman Gallery, London; Fortes D'Aloia & Gabriel, São Paulo and Sikkema Jenkins & Co, New York. Collection of Fondazione Sandretto Re Rebaudengo per l'Arte
104	© Otobong Nkanga; Courtesy of Otobong Nkanga
106	Unsplash
108	Westend61 GmbH/Alamy
110	Dreamstime
112	Klaus Littman, *FOR FOREST – The Unending Attraction of Nature*, 2019. © Klaus Littman
114	Jarmo Piironen/Alamy; Jon G. Fuller/VWPics/Alamy
116	Marshmallow Laser Feast in collaboration with Andres Roberts and James Bulley, *Sanctuary of the Unseen Forest*, 2022. © Marshmallow Laser Feast, Andres Roberts and James Bulley